JESUS HIMSELF

JESUS HIMSELF

The Story of the Resurrection
– from the Garden Tomb to
the Mount of Olives

MARCUS L. LOANE

THE BANNER OF TRUTH TRUST

THE BANNER OF TRUTH TRUST
3 Murrayfield Road, Edinburgh EH12 6EL, UK
P.O. Box 621, Carlisle, PA 17013, USA

*

© Marcus L. Loane 2007

ISBN-10: 0 85151 948 2
ISBN-13: 978 0 85151 948 7

*

All royalties from the sale of this book will go
to the Langham Partnership International

*

Typeset in 11/16 pt Adobe Caslon at the
Banner of Truth Trust, Edinburgh

Printed in the USA by
Versa Press, Inc.,
East Peoria, IL

CONTENTS

The chapters that follow are for me part of a well-loved and life-long pilgrimage. They hardly break any new ground: in the main they simply revise what has been written before. The Resurrection narratives are always fresh and lovely, full of heart-warming fascination. I could easily adapt the language employed by John Bunyan in another connection. Would that I had been there in the early morning when Jesus first appeared! How my heart would have leapt for joy: and how I would have cried 'Rabboni!' No; that would not have been enough: it would have been that later over-whelming confession:

You are my Lord:
You are my God!

Marcus L. Loane

FOREWORD

The wonder and glory of the Resurrection are far greater than we can ever conceive. That great drama took place in the silent tomb a great while before it was yet day. No one else was there when God raised Jesus from the dead: no one saw it happen. There was neither man nor angel as a witness in that sacred moment. He emerged from the grave-clothes and left them lying undisturbed on the ledge. He left the tomb while the stone was still in place at the mouth of the sepulchre. It was later when an earth-quake shook the site and the stone was rolled away. When the women arrived, the guard had fled and they found the tomb empty. The grave-clothes were there; angel watchers were there; but him they did not see.

But no one had seen how he awoke from the sleep of death in newness of life. All that was mortal had put on immortality: death was swallowed up in victory. And it was in his risen glory that he made himself known to his disciples.

There was repeated emphasis on the fact that he did rise from the grave on 'the third day'. This lapse of three days after his death on the cross had been clearly foretold. Jesus himself had said that no sign would be given to that generation save the sign of Jonah. Just as Jonah had been three days in the belly of the great fish, so he would be three days in the darkness of the tomb. He had told the Twelve that he would die, 'and be raised on the third day' (*Matt.* 20:19). After his death, the Pharisees remembered that he had said 'while he was still alive, 'After three days . . .' (*Matt.* 27:63). Time was measured from sunset to sunset: 'there was evening and there was morning, one day' (*Gen.* 1:5, NASB). 'The third day' and 'after three days' were more or less general expressions of time. Jewish practice was to count part of a day as though it were the whole. He was laid in the tomb before sunset, remained there throughout the Sabbath, and rose early on the third day. He was truly dead: his body was laid to rest: then, on 'the first day of the week',

> *He arose! He arose!*
> *Hallelujah! Christ arose!*

I

ST JOHN THE DIVINE

'And he saw, and believed' (John 20:8).

Now on the first day of the week Mary Magdalene came to the tomb early, while it was still dark, and saw that the stone had been taken away from the tomb. [2] So she ran and went to Simon Peter and the other disciple, the one whom Jesus loved, and said to them, 'They have taken the Lord out of the tomb, and we do not know where they have laid him.' [3] So Peter went out with the other disciple, and they were going toward the tomb. [4] Both of them were running together, but the other disciple outran Peter and reached the tomb first. [5] And stooping to look in, he saw the linen cloths lying there, but he did not go in. [6] Then Simon Peter came, following him, and went into the tomb. He saw the linen cloths lying there, [7] and the face cloth, which had been on Jesus' head, not lying with the linen cloths but folded up in a place by itself. [8] Then the other disciple, who had reached the tomb first, also went in, and he saw and believed; [9] for as yet they did not understand the Scripture, that he must rise from the dead. [10] Then the disciples went back to their homes (*John* 20:1–10).

Mary Magdalene, with two or three other women, had stood near the cross to the very end: they had seen how the body had been lowered to the ground and wrapped in a long linen shroud. They had followed Joseph and Nicodemus to the new rock-hewn tomb where the body was laid. Then very early on the morning of the third day they had made their way back to the tomb. Their hope was that they would be able to anoint and embalm those sacred limbs. They were taken aback to discover that the stone had been rolled away and that the guard had fled. No doubt they came and looked inside the tomb, only to be staggered when they found it empty. What had become of the body? How were they to account for the fact that it had vanished? While the others lingered near the tomb, Mary at once thought of Peter and John in the city: she ran as fast as she could to find them in the house where they had taken His mother. 'They have taken the Lord out of the tomb, and we do not know where they have laid him' (*John* 20:2). She was gravely disturbed, full of alarm, and in a state of the utmost anxiety.

Peter and John felt at once that they had to go and see for themselves what had happened: 'So Peter went out with the other disciple, and they were going toward the tomb' (20:3). It was Peter who took the lead, and at first they ran side by side: but Peter was the older man, a man with a troubled conscience, and he began to flag. So John was the first to arrive: the other women had gone: the angels were out of sight: he lost all sense of haste in the unhurried atmosphere as he stood at the door. His whole being was charged with a growing sense of awe and wonder as he stooped down so as to look into the vault where the body had lain. His next step might well have been the normal impulse to go inside: but he did not: he was restrained at the very threshold by sheer surprise. What he saw was the grave-clothes: and not only that: he saw the way they were 'lying'. That word *lying* was used three times (20:5, 6, 7), and is the key to this very human drama.

It was not as though John had come on purpose to look for the grave-clothes. It had never occurred to him that he would find them there at all. It would be as hard to account for what was there as to explain what was not there. But that was not all: there was something unusual, totally different, from what one would expect. That was the way in which the long shroud lay: its position and arrangement were so unusual. The long loose folds were still *lying* at full length on the ledge where the body had been. They were *lying* in the shape which they had assumed when wrapped round the body. The myrrh and aloes, which had been sprinkled between its folds, were still in place. Their weight might have depressed the shroud, but only a little. There was no sign of disorder. The grave-clothes had not been folded up, nor dropped on the floor, nor flung aside: they lay just as they had been when they were wrapped round his body: they were simply *lying* on the slab with fold on fold in perfect order: no human hand nor angel touch had been at work: yet the body itself had gone.

Peter must have been close on John's heels and would arrive a few moments later: 'Then Simon Peter came, following him, and went into the tomb' (20:6). This was the man who at other times was in so much haste to reach the Lord on sea or land: no one was less likely to stand and muse when there was a call for action. While John was still absorbed in a mood of thoughtful wonder, Peter went straight into the tomb: he *saw* the grave-clothes as they lay, fixed his eyes on them, trying to read the riddle. Like John, he saw at once that the shroud was empty: the body had vanished. But just as John had sensed, Peter saw that there was something strange in that scene. It was more than the fact that the shroud was empty: it was the way its folds were *lying*. There was indeed something special that caught and held the eye. But there was more than that because he saw something else that John could not see.

What he saw was how the head-cloth lay rolled up apart from the grave-clothes in its own place. There was the shroud, still in the shape of his body, stretched out at full length along the ledge of rock. But the cloth for his head lay just apart on a slightly raised shelf like a kind of pillow. That cloth had been rolled round his head just as the shroud had been wrapped round his body. But the strangest feature of that head-cloth required a rare word to describe how it appeared. The grave-clothes were *lying* by themselves on the lower level: the head-cloth was *lying* by itself on a slightly higher level. But there were no spices to flatten or depress the head-cloth as in the case of the grave-clothes. The folds had not caved in: it still bore the shape it had taken when wound round his head. That was not an easy thing to describe: what the eye saw would be clearer than what words could convey. There it lay, not with the grave-clothes but by itself, still rolled and round in shape and form. It was just as it had been when Joseph and Nicodemus laid him to rest: no human hand nor angel touch had been at work: yet the body itself had gone.

John soon followed Peter into the tomb where he saw those unique features with his own eyes. 'Then the other disciple . . . also went in, and he saw and believed' (20:8). There lay the grave-clothes, a little depressed, but in perfect order, with not a grain of spice displaced. There lay the head-cloth, a little apart, still in perfect order, with not a roll disturbed. John not only saw the shroud and head-cloth, but he suddenly understood their significance. *'And he saw and believed'*: there was visual perception; there was intelligent understanding.

There had been no lifeless body for foes to steal or friends to take away: he had emerged from the grave-clothes just as he would pass through the stone. John had not hitherto grasped the Scriptures which had foretold that he would rise again. But now a throng of memories half-subdued and of prophecies half-absorbed would crowd his mind: the body gone, the grave-clothes, the head-cloth were a silent witness to the mighty fact of resurrection. It was enough: 'Then the disciples went back to their own homes' (20:10).

2

MARY MAGDALENE

Jesus said to her, "Mary"' (John 20:16).

But Mary stood weeping outside the tomb, and as she wept she stooped to look into the tomb. [12] And she saw two angels in white, sitting where the body of Jesus had lain, one at the head and one at the feet. [13] They said to her, 'Woman, why are you weeping?' She said to them, 'They have taken away my Lord, and I do not know where they have laid him.' [14] Having said this, she turned around and saw Jesus standing, but she did not know that it was Jesus. [15] Jesus said to her, 'Woman, why are you weeping? Whom are you seeking?' Supposing him to be the gardener, she said to him, 'Sir, if you have carried him away, tell me where you have laid him, and I will take him away.' [16] Jesus said to her, 'Mary.' She turned and said to him in Aramaic, 'Rabboni!' (which means Teacher). [17] Jesus said to her, 'Do not cling to me, for I have not yet ascended to the Father; but go to my brothers and say to them, "I am ascending to my Father and your Father, to my God and your God."' [18] Mary Magdalene went and announced to the disciples, 'I have seen the Lord' — and that he had said these things to her (*John* 20:11–18).

English literature does not often excel the chaste beauty of this passage in language and feeling. Sentence follows sentence with scarcely a connecting particle until it reaches the end.

Peter and John had left the tomb and the other women had already gone their way. But Mary had followed the two men back to the garden where she lingered near the tomb. The shock of that death on the cross had plunged her into a grief that was close to despair. Her tears were the only outlet for a sorrow that lay too deep for words. 'But . . . as she wept, she stooped to look into the tomb' (*John* 20:11). Her eyes may have been dim with tears, but she soon saw that she was not alone. It was not the grave-clothes nor the head-cloth on that cold ledge which held her gaze: it was the two angels in white, one at the head and one at the foot of that ledge where the body had lain. They had appeared to the other women after Mary had run on her errand to Peter and John; neither Peter nor John had seen them, but Mary at once became aware of their presence.

Mary looked at them in silent contemplation: it was they who broke the silence: 'They said to her, "Woman, why are you weeping?"' (20:13). A gentle query. They did not tell her what they had told the other women, but they spoke with gentle understanding. *'Woman'*, they said: that was neither cold nor aloof, but a term of courtesy and dignity. But she felt no wonder at the sight of angel faces nor the sound of angel voices: she was far too obsessed with grief because she did not know what had become of his body. She could only respond with a troubled repetition of her words to Peter and John (cf. 20:2). 'She said to them, "They have taken away my Lord, and I do not know where they have laid him"' (20:13).

Those words had gone round and round in her mind until she could think of nothing else. There were only two slight variations, but they were not without significance. Now she spoke of *my* Lord rather than of *the* Lord, and she used the pronoun *I* rather than *we:* she was blind with sorrow; her loss was so personal that all thought of others was forgotten.

That brief exchange came to an end, as a conversation which had nothing further to yield: 'Having said this, she turned around and saw Jesus standing' (20:14). She had stooped down; then she straightened herself; now she turned around to the garden. What made her turn at that precise moment? The Greek text is emphatic. It was not the aimless movement of one whom the angels could not impress. Had she heard a muffled footfall? Had she even seen a fleeting shadow? Chrysostom imagined that some gesture on the part of the two angels caused her to turn around. It may have been so: nothing would have been more real or life-like.

And turn she did: she turned right round; it brought her face to face with Jesus. Her eyes would look into his eyes: she saw him in his risen glory: but 'she did not know that it was Jesus' (20:14). One who had seen angels without alarm saw him as a stranger without concern; recognition failed her because she was in search of one who was alive, as if he were still dead.

Mary had heard the first words to fall from the lips of the risen Saviour: 'Jesus said to her, "Woman, why are you weeping? Whom are you seeking?"' (20:15). He did not wait to see if she would unfold her grief to him: he simply spoke to her as the angels had done. But he spoke in a way that went far beyond a mere expression of sympathy. His first gentle query was identical with that of the angels, but the next words went much further.

But how could a stranger have known the real nature of her secret longing? She offered no answer to his question because a new thought had taken hold of her mind. 'Sir', she said, 'if you have carried him away, tell me where you have laid him' (20:15). Perhaps he was the keeper of the garden; perhaps he knew what had happened. Perhaps he had himself moved the body elsewhere once the Sabbath was past. The pronoun she employed simply assumed that he knew what she meant. Hers was only the strength of a woman, but if she could find him, she would 'take him away' (20:15).

The Lord Jesus had time to mark her tears and read her mind before he spoke again. 'Jesus said to her, "Mary"' (20:16); only one word, but that word would tell her all she needed to know. He spoke in the familiar dialect of Nazareth and Galilee to awaken her memory; and he called her *Mariam,* which was the equivalent of the Greek *Maria* (see 19:25). But there was more, for the very accent of his voice had survived the pains of mortality and death: that name, spoken with that accent, was a word of exceeding tenderness. He had addressed her before as *Woman,* a term of respect such as any man might use. But that was like the voice of a stranger and it awoke no special response. *Mariam* was like the voice of a shepherd who knows his sheep and calls each one by name. Not a glimmer of hope had shone in her soul only a moment or two before. But the tender longing and the vivid accent in that word would tell her as nothing else could do who it was that spoke: for who else could call her by her name in her own native *patois* as he did now?

Mary had begun to turn away when his voice caught her and made her turn again:

> She turned and said to him in Aramaic, 'Rabboni!' (which means Teacher) (20:16).

The word *Woman* had failed to evoke anything more than the word *Sir* in reply (20:15). But her own name, *Mary*, spoke to her heart and called forth her ardent cry, *Rabboni*. Like him she spoke in the familiar dialect of Magdala and Galilee as in the days of old: and the Evangelist was careful to give the Greek equivalent for her form of address. The strict meaning of that vernacular term *Rabboni* was the word *Teacher* or *Master*, but that homely form of address was more personal than the ordinary term *Rabbi*. It was the only time this word was used as a form of address to him after that first resurrection morning, no doubt because it lacked the full sense of lordship which was afterwards understood. But it was the cry of one who had been rescued from the edge of despair, and she poured out all the pent-up love in her heart in that cry of rapture.

3

CERTAIN WOMEN

'And behold, Jesus met them and said, "Greetings!"'
(Matt. 28:9).

Now after the Sabbath, toward the dawn of the first day of the week, Mary Magdalene and the other Mary went to see the tomb. ² And behold, there was a great earthquake, for an angel of the Lord descended from heaven and came and rolled back the stone and sat on it. ³ His appearance was like lightning, and his clothing white as snow. ⁴ And for fear of him the guards trembled and became like dead men. ⁵ But the angel said to the women, 'Do not be afraid, for I know that you seek Jesus who was crucified. ⁶ He is not here, for he has risen, as he said. Come, see the place where he lay. ⁷ Then go quickly and tell his disciples that he has risen from the dead, and behold, he is going before you to Galilee; there you will see him. See, I have told you.' ⁸ So they departed quickly from the tomb with fear and great joy, and ran to tell his disciples. ⁹ And behold, Jesus met them and said, 'Greetings!' And they came up and took hold of his feet and worshipped him. ¹⁰ Then Jesus said to them, 'Do not be afraid; go and tell my brothers to go to Galilee, and there they will see me' (*Matt.* 28: 1–10).

But on the first day of the week, at early dawn, they went to the tomb, taking the spices they had prepared. ² And they found the stone rolled away from the tomb, ³ but when they went in they did not find the body of the Lord Jesus. ⁴ While they were perplexed about this, behold, two men stood by them in dazzling apparel. ⁵ And as they were frightened and bowed their faces to the ground, the men said to them, 'Why do you seek the living among the dead? ⁶ He is not here, but has risen. Remember how he told you, while he was still in Galilee, ⁷ that the Son of Man must be delivered into the hands of sinful men and be crucified and on the third day rise.' ⁸ And they remembered his words, ⁹ and returning from the tomb they told all these things to the eleven and to all the rest. ¹⁰ Now it was Mary Magdalene and Joanna and Mary the mother of James and the other women with them who told these things to the apostles, ¹¹ but these words seemed to them an idle tale, and they did not believe them (*Luke* 24:1–11).

A few faithful women who had stood near the cross then saw where his body was laid to rest. Their last sight of the tomb that day was when the stone was rolled to the mouth of the grave. Their vigil had ended when the sun went down and the Sabbath began. Some time after nightfall on the Sabbath itself they had gone out to buy spices to anoint and embalm the body. Then just before dawn on the third day, the two Marys with Joanna and Salome set out for the tomb: they knew that the folds of the shroud had been sprinkled with spices by Nicodemus. But there had been no time to anoint the body itself in the way that love would dictate. And it was with this in mind that they had set out, though they wondered what would happen when they arrived.

They were to be amazed when they found that the stone had been rolled back so that the tomb was open. But there was more to come: 'when they went in they did not find the body of the Lord Jesus' (*Luke* 24:3). A few moments would pass while they stood lost in thought: then Mary Magdalene left them: she hurried back to the city to tell Peter and John that the body was no longer there.

While the other women stood there, bewildered and uncertain, there was a fresh surprise. 'While they were perplexed about this, behold, two men stood by them in dazzling apparel' (24:4). The presence of angels might well fill them with awe, but their fears were quickly dispelled: 'Do not be afraid', one of the angels said, 'for I know that you seek Jesus who was crucified' (*Matt.* 28:5). They had come in search of one who was dead: they did not dream that he had left the tomb alive. It was just as he had foretold: 'He is not here; for he has risen, as he said' (28:6). They were welcome to see for themselves how things were: 'Come, see the place where he lay' (28:6). There was the ledge where his body had lain and there were the empty grave-clothes.

Perhaps there was no more than a brief pause before they were recalled to the present. 'Then go quickly, and tell his disciples that he has risen from the dead, and behold, he is going before you to Galilee; there you will see him. See, I have told you' (28:7). Such words would help them to collect their thoughts as they took in the astonishing significance of what they had seen and heard.

They lost no time, but where were they to find the disciples? 'So they departed quickly from the tomb with fear and great joy, and ran to tell his disciples' (28:8). Peter and John were somewhere in Jerusalem and it was to Jerusalem that Mary Magdalene had run. But where were the others? They had hardly dared to return, once they had forsaken him and fled. It seems probable that they were at Bethany where friends would keep them in touch.

Therefore while Peter and John left the city to run towards the tomb, the women left the tomb to run in the opposite direction. This would explain why the women did not meet Peter and John as they made their way to the tomb. They did not stay long, but 'went back to their homes' (*John* 20:10). Mary followed them back to the sepulchre, but the other women had gone. She lingered in the garden where she soon came face to face with Jesus. She was then sent to tell the others what she had seen and heard. This took her back to Peter and John while the women were still on their way.

Mary Magdalene dropped out of the story at that point and the focus rested on the other women: 'And behold, Jesus met them and said, "Greetings!" And they came up and . . . worshipped him' (*Matt.* 28:9). Jesus, who came and went at will in his risen body, intercepted them by the way. And his greeting was the normal word of salutation: *'All Hail!'* (AV, see *Matt.* 26:49; 27:29). That was a word of the purest joy for those who heard it on the resurrection morning. For it was an event that would far exceed all that the angels had led them to anticipate. Afterwards perhaps they would remember what he had said on the eve of his death. 'I will see you again and your hearts will rejoice, and no one will take your joy from you' (*John* 16:22). What did they do? They came, and knelt at his feet, and clasped them in awe and adoration. Not that they had to be convinced that he was real: it was the sheer joy of knowing that he was alive. They knew him; they loved him; he had appeared to them even before he was seen of the Twelve. And their hearts overflowed with a sense of wonder that no words could express.

Jesus did not allow them to linger: their joy had to express itself in prompt obedience. 'Do not be afraid', he said; 'go and tell my brothers to go to Galilee, and there they will see me' (28:10). This was just a limited commission, but it was one which they could fulfil. They were sent to the Twelve; it would be for the Twelve to be sent to the world (see *Mark* 16:15).

But his words were much more than a simple repetition of the angel's message (*Matt.* 28:7). They took up the solemn affirmation which he had made on the eve of his death. God would smite the shepherd and would scatter the sheep: but the shepherd would rise again: 'But after I am raised up', he had gone on to say, 'I will go before you to Galilee' (26:32). What if Galilee were the home of rude and unlettered sons of the soil and the sea? And what if the people were of partly Gentile descent and spoke a crude provincial dialect? It was in 'Galilee of the Gentiles' that a great light had first begun to shine (4:12–17). And there they would see him, in the land of their birth, and home, and work, and call. Did those women go on their way while he followed them with his eyes? Perhaps. Did he vanish from their sight while they still knelt by the wayside? Perhaps. We cannot tell; but they wasted no time to do as he had told them.

But it was 'while they were going' that a totally different set of events had begun to evolve (28:11). It is only in Luke's account that we learn the sequel to their early morning experience: 'And returning from the tomb they told all these things to the eleven and to all the rest' (*Luke* 24:9). However, what they said carried no more weight than a tale of make-believe for men who would not credit the truth: 'But these words seemed to them an idle tale, and they did not believe them' (24:11).

But the disciples on the road to Emmaus confessed that they were more telling than had at first appeared:

'Some women of our company amazed us. They were at the tomb early in the morning, and . . . came back saying that they had even seen a vision of angels, who said that he was alive' (24:22–23). The whole story is a transcript from life; its great value is that it tells just what happened on that resurrection morning.

4

SIMON PETER

'But Peter . . . went home marvelling at what had happened' (Luke 24:12).

But on the first day of the week, at early dawn, they went to the tomb, taking the spices they had prepared. [2] And they found the stone rolled away from the tomb, [3] but when they went in they did not find the body of the Lord Jesus. [4] While they were perplexed about this, behold, two men stood by them in dazzling apparel. [5] And as they were frightened and bowed their faces to the ground, the men said to them, 'Why do you seek the living among the dead? [6] He is not here, but has risen. Remember how he told you, while he was still in Galilee, [7] that the Son of Man must be delivered into the hands of sinful men and be crucified and on the third day rise.' [8] And they remembered his words, [9] and returning from the tomb they told all these things to the eleven and to all the rest. [10] Now it was Mary Magdalene and Joanna and Mary the mother of James and the other women with them who told these things to the apostles, [11] but these words seemed to them an idle tale, and they did not believe them. [12] But Peter rose and ran to the tomb; stooping and looking in, he saw the linen cloths by themselves; and he went home marvelling at what had happened (*Luke* 24:1–12).

Peter's state of mind on the eve of the cross must have been one of near despair: he *wept* (*Luke* 22:62) in loneliness and bitterness: the tears of one who was broken-hearted. Where was he when daylight came and they led Jesus out to die on Calvary? All he could think of was the fact that his last words in the hearing of Jesus were words of blasphemy and denial. It was impossible for him to make his way back, kneel at his feet, and plead for forgiveness. He was haunted by guilt and shame: there was nothing to relieve his distress as that day dragged on to an end.

Then at last the body was removed from the cross, wrapped in a shroud and laid in a grave. But he was still in the depths of sorrow: grief bowed his head and wrung his heart. If ever any man's faith was likely to fail, he was that man: what hope was there for him? But there was one small ray of hope which stole through the darkness. 'Simon, Simon,' Jesus had said, 'behold, Satan demanded to have you, that he might sift you (plural) like wheat, but I have prayed for you (singular) that your faith may not fail' (*Luke* 22:31–32).

It would seem that Peter remained as close to John as he could when the shadows fell that evening. It may only have been through that friendship that he did not succumb to a fatal despair. The two men were still in Jerusalem on the third day when they were startled by Mary Magdalene: 'They have taken the Lord out of the tomb, and we do not know where they have laid him' (*John* 20:2). Peter did not know what to think, but he sprang into action at once. He 'rose and ran to the tomb' (*Luke* 24:12); but he did not run alone: John ran with him.

Did they run side by side? Perhaps Peter was in the lead: hope and fear would mingle to quicken his steps. They would leave the city by its gate on the north from which it was barely a hundred yards to the garden. But as they drew closer, Peter began to flag and it was left for John to forge ahead. Was it because Peter's troubled conscience held him back the nearer they came? He was in a state of turmoil, slowed down by the burden of guilt, full of doubt and fear. When he arrived, John was standing at the door of the tomb; what would Peter do?

Peter's only object was to confirm Mary's report that the tomb was empty: 'Stooping and looking in, he saw the linen cloths by themselves' (24:12). It was not as though he had come in search of them; it had never occurred to him that he would find them. But there on the ledge of rock lay the shroud with all its folds still intact. He saw what John had seen; then he did what John had not done: he went inside the tomb. Once he crossed the threshold to stand inside, he saw what could not be seen from the doorway. He saw that the cloth which had been wrapped round the head was still lying in its own place.

Unless there were something unusual in what he saw, further comment would have been pointless. But he saw the linen clothes 'laid by themselves' (24:12, AV), and the head-cloth 'in a place by itself' (*John* 20:7). Neither shroud nor head-cloth had been scattered round the tomb as though thrown aside. They were stretched in perfect order along the ledge of rock where the body had lain. Peter saw it all and stood in wonder; he did not know how to read their secret.

Peter could not solve the riddle of the grave-clothes, but he saw that there was something unique, 'and he went home marvelling at what had happened' (*Luke* 24:12). Meanwhile, even before Peter and John, there were others who had been at the tomb. They too had found the tomb empty. The body had vanished, but two angels were there. 'Do not be afraid,' they were told; 'for I know that you seek Jesus who was crucified' (*Matt.* 28:5). They had come in search of one who was dead. Little did they know that he had left the tomb alive. But it was just as he had foretold: 'He is not here, for he has risen, as he said' (28:6). They could see for themselves the place where the body had lain and the grave-clothes which still remained.

Perhaps there was a brief pause while they were lost in awe and wonder: then the angel went on to say: 'But go, tell his disciples and Peter, that he is going before you into Galilee. There you will see him' (*Mark* 16:7). *'And Peter':* He was singled out from all the others: there was a special word for him: tell . . . *Peter*. What ineffable kindness and insight filled that message for that one man!

What happened next? They would waste no time in doing what they were told: 'They departed quickly from the tomb with fear and great joy, and ran to tell his disciples' (*Matt.* 28:8). But what they had to say seemed no better than an idle tale when they first arrived; nevertheless it seems to have been more telling than had at first appeared. 'Moreover, some women of our company amazed us. They were at the tomb early in the morning, and when they did not find his body, they came back saying that they had even seen a vision of angels, who said that he was alive' (*Luke* 24:22–23).

Then what about Peter? He must have left Jerusalem to rejoin the other disciples wherever they were.

He must have heard how he had been singled out for special mention: what would that imply? But it was like a gleam of hope while time wore slowly away until late afternoon. Then at some point towards evening, the Lord appeared to him; we know not where, nor what was said. We learn of it only through the excited utterance of those who had yet to see him: 'The Lord has risen indeed', words that burst from their lips, 'and has appeared to Simon!' (24:34).

Peter must have hastened to rejoin the others, penitent, chastened, forgiven, thankful. He told them just enough, but the details remain veiled in silence: too personal, too intimate. He had found the others in a private room somewhere in Jerusalem. The doors were shut but the room must have been alive with the hum of eager expectation.

Then came Jesus. There was neither sign nor sound in advance of his coming. They had no time to ask how or whence he came; they were simply aware of his presence. Then in that deep hush of wonder, they heard him say, 'Peace be with you' (*John* 20:19). There was no word of blame for their failure: no reproof, no reproach for those who had fled. That word of peace was still in their ears as he held out his hands and showed them his side.

While their eyes were still on the scars of the cross, he said, 'As the Father has sent me, even so I am sending you' (20:21). That word was for them all. He loved them all alike; there was no distinction between one and another. *And Peter:* Yes, Peter too; there was a special place for him in the heart of the Lord Jesus.

5

EMMAUS

'Jesus himself drew near and went with them'
(Luke 24:15).

That very day two of them were going to a village named Emmaus, about seven miles from Jerusalem, [14] and they were talking with each other about all these things that had happened. [15] While they were talking and discussing together, Jesus himself drew near and went with them. [16] But their eyes were kept from recognizing him. [17] And he said to them, 'What is this conversation that you are holding with each other as you walk?' And they stood still, looking sad. [18] Then one of them, named Cleopas, answered him, 'Are you the only visitor to Jerusalem who does not know the things that have happened there in these days?' [19] And he said to them, 'What things?' And they said to him, 'Concerning Jesus of Nazareth, a man who was a prophet mighty in deed and word before God and all the people, [20] and how our chief priests and rulers delivered him up to be condemned to death, and crucified him. [21] But we had hoped that he was the one to redeem Israel. Yes, and besides all this, it is now the third day since these things happened. [22] Moreover, some women of our company amazed us. They were at the tomb early in the morning, [23] and when they did not find his body, they came back saying that they had even seen a vision of angels, who said that he was alive. [24] Some of those who were with us went to the tomb and found it just as the women had said, but him they did not see.' [25] And he said to them, 'O foolish ones, and slow of heart to believe all that the prophets have spoken! [26] Was it not necessary that the Christ should suffer these things and enter into his glory?' [27] And beginning with Moses and all the Prophets, he interpreted to them in all the Scriptures the things concerning himself.

[28] So they drew near to the village to which they were going. He acted as if he were going farther, [29] but they urged him strongly, saying, 'Stay with us, for it is toward evening and the day is now far spent.' So he went in to stay with them. [30] When he was at table with them, he took the bread and blessed and broke it and gave it to them. [31] And their eyes were opened, and they recognized him. And he vanished from their sight. [32] They said to each other, 'Did not our hearts burn within us while he talked to us on the road, while he opened to us the Scriptures?'

³³ And they rose that same hour and returned to Jerusalem. And they found the eleven and those who were with them gathered together, ³⁴ saying, 'The Lord has risen indeed, and has appeared to Simon!' ³⁵ Then they told what had happened on the road, and how he was known to them in the breaking of the bread (*Luke* 24:13–35).

It was mid-afternoon when the two disciples set out for the village of Emmaus. Why did they leave Jerusalem? Had the apostolic band already begun to disperse? That day had dawned with the resurrection, an event far beyond their wildest dreams: and these two were absorbed in a conversation about 'these things that had happened' (*Luke* 24:14). On the one hand, Jesus had been nailed to the cross: on the other hand, the tomb had been found empty. They were so lost in their own thoughts that they took no notice of what else was going on. They were simply trying to work out some kind of explanation that would account for it all: 'While they were talking and discussing together, Jesus himself drew near and went with them' (24:15). They were still so preoccupied with their own grief that they showed no surprise: 'What is this conversation that you are holding with each other as you walk?' (24:17). They were shocked. *They stood still.* A look of great sadness stole over their faces: but it never occurred to them that this stranger was the very person of whom they were speaking.

Jesus drew near to men at an hour when they were *desperately sad and troubled:* 'Are you the only visitor to Jerusalem who does not know the things that have happened there in these days?' (24:18). It was not as though Jesus had been put to death in secret: the cross stood high over Jerusalem: and the people had thought of him as a prophet who was mighty in deed and word. Yet the chief priests and the rulers had delivered him up to be crucified, a form of death so stark and terrible that they could hardly bear to contemplate it.

Worse still, he was the one whom they believed had been sent to redeem Israel: all their hopes and dreams had been dashed to the ground with his death on the cross. It was as though the fire of faith had burnt out when he bowed his head and died, and the ashes of that fire were as cold as the grave in which his body had been laid.

If he were not the one that should come, to whom were they to look? There was nothing left for which to hope. Sorrow filled their hearts: they were stricken with grief, a grief too deep for tears.

Jesus drew near to men at an hour when they were *grievously hurt and confused:* their sorrow had taken on a darker hue because their faith was at risk. This was now 'the third day' since he had been put to death on the cross. That day began with a visit by a group of women to the tomb in which his body had lain. They found that the stone had been rolled away. The tomb was open. His body had vanished. The disciples were astounded when they were told; but there was more to it than that. They were also told that 'they had even seen a vision of angels, who said that he was alive' (24:23).

Alive! What did that mean? Should they dismiss it as a mere 'idle tale'? (24:11). Peter and John had run to the tomb to see for themselves whether it were true. They 'found it just as the women had said, but him they did not see' (24:24). The idea of resurrection had never crossed their own mental threshold. They did not know what to think. They were more than ever confused.

Jesus drew near to men at a time when they were *dull and slow of heart to believe.* Did they not know that it was necessary for the Christ to suffer before he could enter into his glory? Then he began with Moses and went on through all the prophets to expound the truth about the Christ. He took the key of truth to unlock the Messianic teaching of the Old Testament.

They had heard the Scriptures read every Sabbath in the synagogue, and yet they had never heard scribe or rabbi speak as this stranger now spoke. Who but Jesus could have measured up to such a revelation of all that the Christ should be? Was it not to him that all the Law and the Prophets had borne witness? But they were *slow of heart* to ask themselves who this stranger might be. It was only in the light of after events that they recalled the impact of his testimony. Then they turned one to the other and began to exclaim with mutual surprise, 'Did not our hearts burn within us while he talked to us on the road?' (24:32).

Jesus drew near to men at a time when *their eyes were ready to open*. They had been so absorbed in the conversation that they had lost all sense of time. Almost before they were aware, they found themselves in the outskirts of the village. The sun was low in the sky: the day was far spent; evening was at hand. They had come to the end of their journey, but he let it seem that he had further to go.

They were loath to part with him and they constrained him to come in and lodge with them. A simple meal was prepared and all three would recline round the table. Then 'he took the bread and blessed and broke it and gave it to them' (24:30). The same familiar actions, and in the same sequence, as at the feeding of five thousand and at the Lord's Supper. This was not a miracle like the one, nor a eucharist like the other, but it called up nostalgic memories. They saw something in his manner, just as Mary had heard something in his accent: 'And their eyes were opened, and they recognized him. And he vanished out of their sight' (24:31).

There are all too many today who still follow the path of life with sad and troubled hearts. They had always cherished the idea that somehow God would come to their rescue. But it has not worked out like that; something has gone wrong; they feel let down. What has happened? Is it that God has failed? They are confused, they do not understand.

It is just to people like that that Jesus himself still seeks to draw near. They may not know him at first. It is as though he comes in the guise of a stranger. But he comes in fact as a friend.

He comes as one who knows and cares for them, and his Word will shed fresh rays of light on their confused and troubled minds. If, at the close of the day, they will but ask him to come in and dwell with them, he will respond, and make himself known in the breaking of bread. Their hearts will grow strangely warm as they learn who is their guest: and they will go on their way to declare that 'the Lord has risen indeed!' (24:34).

6

JERUSALEM

'On the evening of that day . . . Jesus came and stood among them and said to them, "Peace be with you"' (John 20:19).

On the evening of that day, the first day of the week, the doors being locked where the disciples were for fear of the Jews, Jesus came and stood among them and said to them, 'Peace be with you.' [20] When he had said this, he showed them his hands and his side. Then the disciples were glad when they saw the Lord. [21] Jesus said to them again, 'Peace be with you. As the Father has sent me, even so I am sending you.' [22] And when he had said this, he breathed on them and said to them, 'Receive the Holy Spirit. [23] If you forgive the sins of anyone, they are forgiven; if you withhold forgiveness from anyone, it is withheld' (John 20:19–23).

That day had been full of troubled rumour, stoked by suspense and surprise. The disciples, in or near Jerusalem, hardly knew what to think or whom to believe. The seal on the stone had been broken, the guard at the tomb had fled, the stone itself had been rolled back, and an angel guard kept watch outside the tomb. The tomb itself was empty, yet not quite empty; the grave-clothes were still there: but where was the body? It had vanished; no one could say what had become of it. Reports had trickled in throughout the day: something incredible had happened, he was alive!

Nightfall found them tense and unsure, alternating between hope and alarm. Those who were within reach of the city had instinctively begun to assemble with each other. Judas was dead. Thomas was off on his own; but ten of the Twelve were there; some others as well. They did not know what to expect, but they felt that something was bound to happen: if he had really appeared to others, surely he would soon make himself known to them.

There had never been a day like that before, but it drew to an end at last: 'On the evening of that day, the first day of the week, the doors being locked ... for fear of the Jews' (*John* 20:19). There is gentle emphasis on the fact that this was now 'the first day of the week'. During that day, Jesus had appeared to Mary, to the women, to Peter, and to the disciples at Emmaus. But when evening came, they were all in a friendly home somewhere in Jerusalem. They were not free from an underlying anxiety: 'the doors being locked', barred and bolted. They were in the heart of that city in which Jesus had been condemned and crucified. Were they safe from the Jews? Who could tell how the rulers would react? Rumours of the resurrection had already begun to circulate in certain quarters. The guard had told the priests of the earthquake and the angel and the vanished body. What would happen if the temple police were to swoop on the disciples? They were nervous enough, but the room was full of excitement and expectation.

Conversation was in full swing until a sudden change caused a deep hush: 'Jesus came and stood among them and said to them, "Peace be with you"' (20:19). He came, when they least thought of it. He came, though the doors were locked. Suddenly, silently, he came, with neither shadow nor footfall to tell of his coming.

John did not say how he came, no doubt because he did not know. He was content simply to state the fact; there was nothing more he could add. He did not say that the doors were thrown open, or even that he came through the door. Jesus had simply stepped into their midst: he was there almost before they were aware of it.

Nor was that all. He not only came; he spoke, and they heard his voice. There was no word of blame, no rebuke, no reproach for their sin and failure. They could hardly forget how they had all forsaken him and fled. But there was no mention of that. His voice fell on their ears; his words were words of peace.

The hush of a profound silence may have lasted for a moment or two. No one had heard him knock; no one had seen him come: but he was there! They saw his face; they heard his voice; but they could hardly take it in. But his very first gesture would confirm that he was 'this same Jesus' (*Acts* 1:11, AV). 'He showed them his hands and his side' (*John* 20:20); they saw the scars of the cross. All the visible evidence of atonement and sacrifice was spread before their eyes. It was enough.

John would forever recall that moment as if it were but yesterday. 'Then the disciples were *glad*', so he wrote, 'when they saw the Lord' (20:20). *Glad:* a word so calm and serene that it totally understates the facts. They were *overjoyed;* overwhelmed with joy, a joy that time could never erode.

Perhaps there is nothing that we so much stand in need of today as for Jesus to look into our eyes and speak to our hearts, 'Peace be with you.'

Note on John 20:19–23

It is easy to read through this passage without pausing to reflect on its structure. That leaves one to wonder why the salutation of peace occurs twice in so short a space. Was it redundant? Or was there some special underlying significance?

I think there was: the words were an integral part of the literary structure of this passage. It falls into two halves, and there is a distinct break between each half. Each half began with the greeting of peace: 'Peace be with you'; 'Peace be with you' (20:19, 21). That greeting was followed by a natural formula as an introduction to the next point: 'When he had said this' (20:20); 'And when he had said this' (20:22). After what had been said, there was an immediate action of a practical character.

In the first half, it was this: 'He showed them his hands and his side' (20:20). In the second half, it was quite different: 'He breathed on them' (20:22).

In each case that set the scene for something further of exceptional significance. First there was the effect on those who were present: 'Then the disciples were glad when they saw the Lord' (20:20). Then there was the profound and mysterious saying: 'Receive the Holy Spirit' (20:22).

So let the whole passage be read with a brief pause in the middle as the literary structure dictates, and the meaning or purpose or value of the double salutation of peace is perfectly clear.

7

THOMAS, CALLED THE TWIN
(PART ONE)

'I will never believe' (John 20:25).

Now Thomas, one of the Twelve, called the Twin, was not with them when Jesus came. ²⁵ So the other disciples told him, 'We have seen the Lord.' But he said to them, 'Unless I see in his hands the mark of the nails, and place my finger into the mark of the nails, and place my hand into his side, I will never believe' (*John* 20:24–25).

Thomas was coupled with Matthew in each list of the Twelve whom the Lord called and ordained. But the little we know of him apart from this is all found in St John's Gospel. It was Thomas who saw that a journey to Bethany after the death of Lazarus would be fraught with danger; nevertheless he was resolved to go on with Jesus in spite of his own deep foreboding. 'Let us also go', he said to the rest of the Twelve, 'that we may die with him' (*John* 11:16). It was Thomas who broke with the Lord's declaration that he would be going to his Father. He could not understand what Jesus meant and he blurted out his anxious query: 'Lord', he said, 'we do not know where you are going. How can we know the way?' (14:5). The same spirit of unease and sorrow darkened his mind after the cross: he thought that the reports of the resurrection were too good to be true. His own profound sense of loss and sorrow made him slow to believe: it was in fact hard for him to believe just what he most longed to believe.

Where was Thomas on that resurrection evening? Why was he not with all the others? 'Now Thomas, one of the Twelve, called the Twin, was not with them when Jesus came' (20:24). Neither Jesus nor the rest of the Twelve found fault with him for his absence. But that absence was not accidental: he was not there because he had chosen to be alone. There is not the slightest hint that would point to where he might have gone. But there were signs that the close-knit circle of disciples had begun to break up. In mid-afternoon, two of the disciples had left the others and had set out for Emmaus. It may have been soon afterwards that Peter had gone out to be alone. Jesus himself had forewarned them that this would happen as it was written: 'I will strike the shepherd, and the sheep of the flock will be scattered' (*Matt.* 26:31). There may have been a variety of motives that prompted Thomas to seek solitude. There was indeed something in his absence that would reflect feelings common to them all.

Thomas must have been much in the mind of all the others that evening. 'So the other disciples told him, "We have seen the Lord"' (*John* 20:25). Was it that self-same night that he returned and met with the others again? Had they gone in search of him? Did he come in soon after Jesus had left? They were still in the first flush of joy and they greeted him with overflowing delight. This was their first recorded utterance on that night of all nights and the tense of the Greek verb is emphatic! They spoke, not once, nor twice, but again and again, as if it could not be too often. It was continued, repeated testimony: they kept on saying what they knew. They had *seen* the Lord; they had *seen* the nail-prints in his hands and his feet. Those scars were the *stigmata* which proved beyond all doubt that his body was real; they had not been deceived: this was not a spirit, nor a ghost, nor some kind of apparition. It was *this same Jesus* who had died on the cross and had then been laid in the grave.

How did Thomas respond to that joyous outburst from all his friends? 'Unless I see in his hands the mark of the nails, and place my finger . . .' (20:25). This dogmatic rejection of their testimony was as harsh and final as words could make it. They were his friends, men who could have had no earthly reason to pretend or deceive. They were the last of men to mock his faith in what to him was so sacred.

But he was as stubborn as they had been when they would not believe what they were told. They had dismissed the news which the women had brought as no better than an idle tale (*Luke* 24:11). There was something in him that held Thomas back in spite of his deepest longing. He had a kind of glum independence that made him speak brusquely. What they had seen, he must see for himself; he asked for no more and no less. Did they believe before they saw the print of the nails? Could he believe unless he saw it too? He was wrong, but who that knows his own heart will not say that it was very human?

Thomas had fixed his mind on the scars left by the nails and the spear: 'Unless I see . . . and place my hand into his side, I will never believe' (20:25). Thomas had none of the Sadducean outlook which Jesus had condemned: 'Unless you see signs and wonders', he had said, 'you will not believe' (4:48). But the others had been allowed proofs that were not dissimilar to what Thomas required. 'See my hands and my feet, that it is I myself. Touch me, and see. For a spirit does not have flesh and bones as you see that I have' (*Luke* 24:39). Thomas may well have shaped his words in line with what they had told him, and his obstinacy stood out in his repeated emphasis on the *stigmata*. 'The mark of the nails . . . the mark of the nails': he wanted the evidence of sight. 'Place my finger . . . place my hand': he wanted as well the evidence of touch. Thomas wanted to be able to *look* and *feel*, just as all the others had done. He wanted more than their verbal testimony: he wanted his own intimate experience.

Thomas was a man who sought proof beyond all doubt; nothing else would suffice. He could hardly have been more blunt: 'Unless I shall see . . . I will never believe.' This attitude was underlined in the Greek text with a peculiar emphasis. It was enforced by the use of a double negative: 'I will *never* believe.' He did not say, 'If I see, then I will believe': he said, 'Unless I see, nothing will make me believe.' He made it clear that for him seeing would be believing; there could be no other way. Thomas had cut himself off from all the others so as to mourn and brood alone. He was in the vice-like grip of the kind of doubt that is close to despair. There are many today who like him have heard of Jesus by the hearing of the ear, but they do not believe because they have not seen him with their own eyes. There is only one place where such doubt can be resolved and that is at his feet: until then they need to cry with desperate earnestness, 'Lord . . . help thou mine unbelief' (*Mark* 9:24, AV).

8

THOMAS, CALLED THE TWIN
(PART TWO)

'My Lord and my God!' (John 20:28).

Eight days later, his disciples were inside again, and Thomas was with them. Although the doors were locked, Jesus came and stood among them and said, 'Peace be with you.' ²⁷ Then he said to Thomas, 'Put your finger here, and see my hands; and put out your hand, and place it in my side. Do not disbelieve, but believe.' ²⁸ Thomas answered him, 'My Lord and my God!' ²⁹ Jesus said to him, 'Have you believed because you have seen me? Blessed are those who have not seen and yet have believed.' ³⁰ Now Jesus did many other signs in the presence of the disciples, which are not written in this book; ³¹ but these are written so that you may believe that Jesus is the Christ, the Son of God, and that by believing you may have life in his name (*John* 20:26–31).

No one knew in advance when the risen Lord would stand in their midst again. Nor do we know how that week was spent, nor where the Twelve found a lodging. They must have been days of endless joy and wonder for all except Thomas: for him each day would pass slowly while doubt still racked his mind. But he did not leave his brethren again and their certainty must have told on his heart: 'Eight days later, his disciples were inside again, and Thomas was with them' (20:26).

The *eight days* would include the two extremes, so that this was the next Sunday after Easter: the octave for the Passover festival had only ended the day before. Perhaps this was why the disciples had not already left for Galilee as they had been enjoined. Now they had met in the same room behind closed doors just as before. The words *inside . . . again* serve to recall the scene as it was eight days before. Would he now come again for the sake of Thomas? What if nothing were to happen?

What did happen was almost a replay of what had happened before: 'Although the doors were locked, Jesus came and stood among them and said, "Peace be with you"' (20:26). *Jesus came:* and the present tense in the original makes the words ring out with a marked solemnity. It was the same swift and silent advent, with neither shadow nor footfall to tell of his coming. He came as from nowhere; he came as though there were no doors at all; he stood in their midst, and his first word was that word of peace.

Then he turned to Thomas as the man who would not believe until he saw him. He had not sought Thomas while he was still alone, as he had sought Mary and Peter. This was because Thomas had avowed his unbelief in the presence of his brethren. It had been their joyful testimony which he had totally rejected. Therefore he would have to retract his words in their presence and hearing. And that moment had come when the Lord turned to him in the lamplight of that quiet room.

No one else had spoken when he turned to Thomas in an awful silence. 'Put your finger here, and see my hands', he said, 'and put out your hand, and place it in my side. Do not disbelieve, but believe' (20:27). There stood Jesus in his risen glory; there stood Thomas in his sorry turmoil. And he offered Thomas proof in the terms which he had so rashly prescribed. Thomas heard him recite the words of the challenge which he had so rashly thrown out. And his exact knowledge of what Thomas had said was in itself overwhelming.

Then he held out his hands and laid bare his side so that Thomas could see. And he voiced his invitation in the very words which Thomas had used. Thomas was to draw near; he was to come and see; he was to touch and feel. He had asked for the starkest reality and that was what he was offered. There was just the mildest reproof for his earlier unbelief: 'Do not disbelieve, but believe.' With those scars of the cross before his eyes, how could he not believe?

All this took place in the hush of that room while the others looked on. 'Thomas answered him, "My Lord and my God"' (20:28). Did he actually finger those wounds? We are not told, but it is unlikely. His response was so swift and spontaneous that it rules out any further delay. Doubt had vanished at the very sight of Jesus, like mist in the morning sunrise. And his adoring utterance of faith more than matched his vehement expression of doubt.

His suspense had gone; his reserve had dissolved: and he could say like Job, 'I had heard of you by the hearing of the ear, but now my eye sees you' (*Job* 42:5). He knew now how wrong-headed and obstinate had been his refusal to believe. And he was now deeply ashamed of his reckless demand for proof. Whereas the others had been *glad* when they saw the Lord, he was overwhelmed with *awe*. All his pent-up feelings were poured out in that cry of wonder and worship.

There was something akin to simple grandeur in that cry of humble worship. His words were few, but full of glorious certainty: You are my Lord; you are my God! *My Lord:* He who had died on the cross was now alive and would die no more. *My God:* He who had now risen from the grave was revealed as none other than God.

It was as though his heart were to ascend from the thought of Jesus risen to a still more lofty level: and the pronouns, *my . . . my*, invest the words with the glorious certainty of his own faith. It was the most advanced statement of faith ever made by one of the Twelve; it rose to a height and maturity never surpassed in the days of his flesh. Nathanael had said, 'Rabbi, you are the Son of God, you are the King of Israel' (1:49). Peter had said, 'You are the Christ, the Son of the living God' (*Matt.* 16:16). Thomas saw that he was more than *the Christ;* more than *the Son of God*: he was both *Lord* and *God*. And no confession of his deity could have been more reverent or more absolute.

The last word, that lay with Jesus, was for the sake of all future generations: 'Have you believed because you have seen me? Blessed are those who have not seen and yet have believed' (20:29).

The first clause may be read either as a comment or as a question (see also 1:50). The truth at first had seemed like a phantom seen through a haze of doubt: but it shone with glorious certainty once he stood face to face with the risen Lord. However, we cannot see as Thomas once saw; we can only believe what those who did see have told us. But a deeper faith is now called for and a richer blessing now lies in store. Thomas saw the print of the nails: blessed was he; we have not seen and yet believe: still more blessed are we. We cannot reach out our finger to touch him as Thomas could, but we have no need to envy Thomas. Jesus is the one whom having not seen, we love; though we do not now see him, we believe in him and rejoice with joy that is inexpressible and filled with glory (1 *Pet.* 1:8).

NOTE ON JOHN 20:30–31

These two verses are a comment by the Evangelist on the foregoing narrative: they sum up and round off his whole account of the resurrection of the Lord Jesus. They look back over all the events of which he had written, crowned by the glory of the resurrection. 'Now then', he says, 'Jesus did many other signs . . . but these are written so that you may believe' (20:30–31).

He had written his account in order to lead men to believe that Jesus is the Christ, the Son of God. It had reached a noble climax in the words of Thomas: 'My Lord and my God' (20:28). It seems clear that St John meant those words to form a dignified conclusion to the Gospel. What more could he say that would not take something from its graphic impact? It was his own instinct for the effect of the Gospel that made him think like this. And it shaped his sense of climax better than the finest literary skill could have done. It was not his purpose to write a life story in the formal sense of that word; it was simply to place on record the good news that points to 'life in his name' (20:31).

There were seven *signs* which had been chosen to highlight the message of the Gospel, and each *sign* was shown to possess its own special significance in the Gospel. But there were *many other signs* which Jesus had done but which were not mentioned. They were called *signs* because they led men to look below the surface of things. They were like a divine signpost which pointed to a deeper revelation of truth. They were meant to provide some fresh insight into the mysteries of the world we see. But the *signs* which were on record were all meant to point to Jesus so that they might believe.

Jesus was the name that spoke of his humanity and humility; but far more than this, he was *the Christ* who had fulfilled all the hopes of Israel, *the Son of God* who had come to redeem mankind. Many might look for a second Moses or a second David, for another Elijah or another Solomon. But these things were written that men may know that *the Christ* has come. And all to one great end: 'that by believing you may have life in his name' (20:31).

9

GALILEE

'After this Jesus revealed himself again to the disciples by the sea of Tiberias, and he revealed himself in this way' (John 21:1).

After this Jesus revealed himself again to the disciples by the Sea of Tiberias, and he revealed himself in this way. [2] Simon Peter, Thomas (called the Twin), Nathanael of Cana in Galilee, the sons of Zebedee, and two others of his disciples were together. [3] Simon Peter said to them, 'I am going fishing.' They said to him, 'We will go with you.' They went out and got into the boat, but that night they caught nothing.

[4] Just as day was breaking, Jesus stood on the shore; yet the disciples did not know that it was Jesus. [5] Jesus said to them, 'Children, do you have any fish?' They answered him, 'No.' [6] He said to them, 'Cast the net on the right side of the boat, and you will find some.' So they cast it, and now they were not able to haul it in, because of the quantity of fish. [7] That disciple whom Jesus loved therefore said to Peter, 'It is the Lord!' (*John* 21:1–7).

The last words of chapter 20 would have been a perfect ending for the Gospel, but the Evangelist took up his pen once more to add a fresh chapter as a kind of post-script.

The disciples had been told to return to Galilee where they would see him (*Matt.* 28:7, 10). And as soon as the Passover festival came to an end they left Jerusalem for their northern province. 'After this Jesus revealed himself again to the disciples by the Sea of Tiberias' (*John* 21:1).

After this: the usual formula for the resumption of a narrative (see also *John* 3:22; 5:1; 6:1; 7:1). The point of time was not clearly defined, but the disciples were back in Galilee. They were in their old haunts, close to their boats and their nets, drawn to the sea. They were strengthened by the promise that there they would see him, but chafed at the delay.

Seven of them, led by Simon Peter, were all together, perhaps in his own home. There were Thomas and Nathanael, the two sons of Zebedee, and two others, probably Andrew and Philip. They knew that Jesus had risen and their hearts were at one in their longing to be with him. But they did not know how or when he would come and suspense made them crave for activity: 'Simon Peter said to them, "I am going fishing." They said to him, "We will go with you"' (21:3). Peter was the leading spirit in this venture, true to his instinct as a man of action. But most of them had been born and bred by the lake and were at home with all its reefs and shoals. 'They went out and got into the boat, but that night they caught nothing' (21:3). Out on the water, beneath the stars, plying their skills, they could wait with quiet hope for his coming. In that boat, he had sailed: from its bow, he had taught: in its stern, he had slept. Here they had heard him as he stilled the storm; here they had seen him as he walked on the waves. Memories would crowd into their minds as they went to work in the old way. But now, toil as they might, all their efforts were in vain: they caught nothing.

That night: the pronoun is emphatic; it suggests that their failure was exceptional. Their nets were let down and hauled in time and again: but they were always empty. Disappointment was at its peak when a sudden change turned things round. 'Just as day was breaking, Jesus stood on the shore; yet the disciples did not know that it was Jesus' (21:4).

The pale light of dawn had begun to spread over the hills when Jesus came. There was nothing to tell where he had spent the night or whence he had come. The light was just enough for the men in the boat to see someone in the distance, someone who was standing on the narrow margin of beach strewn with shells and pebbles. But that figure was too dim in that grey dawn for them to tell who he was. Preoccupied with toil and worn out with fatigue, they were totally unexpectant. Cold and listless, they had no thought for a stranger: they 'did not know that it was Jesus'. They were like the disciples on the road to Emmaus: 'Their eyes were kept from recognizing him' (*Luke* 24:16). They were no longer on the alert, or their hearts would have leapt for joy; but it never crossed their minds that that far-off solitary figure might be the Lord.

Jesus at once began to forge contact with them through a question of the utmost simplicity: 'Jesus said to them, "Children, do you have any fish?" They answered him, "No"' (21:5). They looked so lacklustre as they trailed the slack mesh behind their boat. But his question was an easy way of putting himself in touch with them. His voice would float across the calm water in the stillness of dawn.

Children, he called: a word that was used much as a word like 'lads' or 'boys'. Chrysostom understood the call as if he were asking if they had fish to sell, but it only suggests something to eat, like fish to eat with bread (see also *John* 6:9).

Was the question meant to imply that he knew they had met with no success? Was it as if he were to say, 'So you have caught nothing?' And their reply came back, just as weary men with empty nets would shout. It was brief, and curt, and blunt: *No!* There was nothing more to say.

This was the great moment when he chose to reveal himself. 'He said to them, "Cast the net on the right side of the boat, and you will find some"' (21:6). Perhaps this would stir vague recollections of how it had all happened once before. And the command was so precise that they never thought to question it. Perhaps this was partly the non-resistance of fatigue, partly the faint hope of success.

Could he see a shoal of fish on the right side which they could not see from the water's level? It was common enough for one boat to make a haul while others a few yards away took nothing: one might strike the shoal which others had missed. Such would be their feelings as they let down their nets for one last haul.

The result was overwhelming: the net was so heavy with fish that they could not pull it in. Did this show

how tired their arms must have been? Yet the net did not break. It was all they could do to bring the boat to shore, dragging the net behind.

One of the seven at least was stirred with a flash of insight to grasp the truth: 'That disciple whom Jesus loved therefore said to Peter, "It is the Lord"' (21:7). John saw nothing which the others could not see just as well. It was not as though his eyes were clearer than theirs, but he perceived what was hidden from them.

It was just as when he had stood beside Peter in the empty tomb on the resurrection morning: the body had gone: the grave-clothes were there: Peter saw and wondered; John 'saw and believed'. So now it was with a sudden flash of insight that John grasped the truth: he knew who it was that stood on the shore. He whispered to Peter, *It is the Lord.* John's first recorded utterance at the beginning of his ministry had been 'Rabbi, where are you staying?' (1:38). A whole world of thought lay between that first *Rabbi* and this recognition of him as the *Lord.* It was Thomas who had first made use of that new designation: *my Lord and my God* (20:28). Now John's spontaneous word to Peter showed how quickly that new title had taken hold.

10

A FIRE OF COALS

'This was now the third time that Jesus was revealed to the disciples after he was raised from the dead' (John 21:14).

When Simon Peter heard that it was the Lord, he put on his outer garment, for he was stripped for work, and threw himself into the sea. [8] The other disciples came in the boat, dragging the net full of fish, for they were not far from the land, but about a hundred yards off. [9] When they got out on land, they saw a charcoal fire in place, with fish laid out on it, and bread. [10] Jesus said to them, 'Bring some of the fish that you have just caught.' [11] So Simon Peter went aboard and hauled the net ashore, full of large fish, 153 of them. And although there were so many, the net was not torn. [12] Jesus said to them, 'Come and have breakfast.' Now none of the disciples dared ask him, 'Who are you?' They knew it was the Lord. [13] Jesus came and took the bread and gave it to them, and so with the fish. [14] This was now the third time that Jesus was revealed to the disciples after he was raised from the dead (*John* 21:7–14).

N othing could have been more life-like than John's whispered revelation, 'It is the Lord' (21:7). But while recognition might be enough for John, action was imperative for Peter. As soon as he heard that it was the Lord who was calling them across the water, 'he put on his outer garment, for he was stripped for work, and threw himself into the sea' (21:7).

He had to act at once, but was partly restrained by nakedness and modesty: he was less than half clad, wearing next to nothing, 'stripped of all but his light under garment'.[1] Therefore he caught up the outer cloak which would be worn on cold nights or in stormy weather, wrapped it round his body, threw himself overboard, and made for the land. Half swimming, half wading, caring not how, his one thought was to reach the Lord, the same impulsive kind of devotion that had once made him leave the boat to meet him on the water. Only an eyewitness would have noted how he put on that cloak just as he was about to leap into the sea, but it was just like him and the circumstances would explain his action.

---

[1] B. F. Westcott, *Commentary on the Gospel of John*, 1881, p. 301.

Peter forgot fish and net, boat and friends, in his haste to be at his side: 'The other disciples came in the boat, dragging the net full of fish' (21:8). It was left to John and the others to handle the situation with the boat and the fish.

They would have to anchor the main boat and transfer to a smaller skiff. This was *the little boat* (21:8, AV), a small craft which was towed astern. They would secure the net, teeming with fish, behind this small boat and tow it to land. Perhaps they beached their boat just when Peter also reached the shore, but they did not haul in the net at once: for the moment the fish were forgotten.

They had been toiling all night and were worn out with disappointment when morning came. But now they were on the tiptoe of a new-found wonder; they were alive with joy.

Not a word was said. The only word had been John's whispered word to Simon Peter: they were simply caught up in a silent concert of awe in the presence of the risen Lord.

Everything was different from all that the disciples might have expected: 'When they got out on land, they saw a charcoal fire in place, with fish laid out on it, and bread' (21:9).

How did Peter greet him when at last he got there? Did the others come and worship? The text passes over such details in silence and turns at once to the next scene. There on the cold pebbles they saw a fire of coals and the food for a meal: who had laid that charcoal fire, and from where had come that fish and that loaf? They were cold, tired, wet and hungry; it was all just what they needed. It would all add to the element of mystery which was the hallmark of his presence. But he would have them bring their own portion as well before the meal began: 'Jesus said to them, "Bring some of the fish that you have just caught"' (21:10). That haul of fish had been netted partly through his guidance, partly through their efforts. So this morning meal was to be furnished partly by him and partly by themselves.

Simon Peter, always headstrong and foremost in action, at once took charge: 'So Simon Peter went aboard and hauled the net ashore, full of large fish' (21:11). The net was still fastened to the ship which lay in shallow water. He hauled it in, laid the fish on the beach, and then began to count them as in the days of old. No doubt six pairs of hands beside his own would help to lay them out: they would all share the thrill of their early calling as that catch was numbered. We can almost hear his voice as he stood counting each fish in turn: *one hundred and fifty-three of them:* a large haul by any standard. Not just a round number: there was finality both in the count and the record. There was the same precision as with the five barley loaves and two small fish to feed *the five thousand* (6:9-13). One other vividly remembered detail arose from the size of that haul with a single cast of the net: in spite of that struggling mass of fish, the net was neither torn nor broken.

Then they heard his voice as he spoke again in the crisp air of that early morning: 'Jesus said to them, "Come and have breakfast." Now none of the disciples dared ask him, "Who are you?"' (21:12). Once before he had offered practical evidence of his reality: he took 'a piece of broiled fish . . . and ate before them' (*Luke* 24:42-43).

Proof of that kind was no longer necessary, but he knew that they were still ill-at-ease. And to relieve their sense of awe, he called them to come and have breakfast. Were they standing at a little distance, held back with mingled awe and wonder? Let them *come.* Were they feeling cold and hungry after that long night on the water? Let them *eat.* No doubt he would approach the fire from the land side as they from the lake side, but no one dared to ask who he was, for they all knew that it was *the Lord*.

The whole scene was allowed to unfold in silence, the silence of unspoken reverence. The long suspense was now over. *The Lord* had come; they were with him.

It was clear, just as at Emmaus, that he was the host and they were his guests: 'Jesus came and took the bread and gave it to them, and so with the fish' (*John* 21:13). The sun came up over the hills and turned the grey waters to gold as he took the bread and the fish, and gave to each man his portion.

Was there just one loaf and one fish, enough for one man, on that fire of coals? Did it increase in his hands as he broke it and gave it to each in turn? We do not know. We are not even told if he also partook of that fish and that bread; enough to know that it was *the Lord* who came to preside at that frugal meal. 'This was now the third time that Jesus was revealed to the disciples after . . .' (21:14). Words that connect this scene with the earlier narratives centred in Jerusalem (see *John* 20:19–23, 26–29). Perhaps their sense of awe was now even greater than on previous occasions, for each successive appearance would tell them that he was nearer to his final glory.

II

THE HEART OF LOVE

'Lord, you know everything; you know that I love you' (John 21:17).

When they had finished breakfast, Jesus said to Simon Peter, 'Simon, son of John, do you love me more than these?' He said to him, 'Yes, Lord; you know that I love you.' He said to him, 'Feed my lambs.' [16] He said to him a second time, 'Simon, son of John, do you love me?' He said to him, 'Yes, Lord; you know that I love you.' He said to him, 'Tend my sheep.' [17] He said to him the third time, 'Simon, son of John, do you love me?' Peter was grieved because he said to him the third time, 'Do you love me?' and he said to him, 'Lord, you know everything; you know that I love you.' Jesus said to him, 'Feed my sheep' (*John* 21:15–17).

I t was early morning by the Sea of Galilee with the sun still rising over the hills. The seven disciples stood in a semicircle round the fire of coals and the frugal meal. They were face to face with the Lord Jesus, lost in silent awe and wonder.

Then one man was singled out and engaged in an intensely personal dialogue. Not one word was said with regard to what lay in the past, but its shadow was the backdrop. Three times in all the Lord would ask the same question; three times Peter had to reply. 'Simon, son of John, do you love me? . . . Yes, Lord; you know that I love you.' But the English text conceals the different shade of meaning in the Greek verbs.[1] Αγαπαω (agapao) spoke of love in its most lofty sense, love born of respect and understanding. Φιλεω (phileo) spoke of love on a much lower level, the warm-hearted affection of a man for his friend. The two verbs used apart were likely to absorb something of each other's meaning: but placed side by side, as in this context, the distinction needs to be carefully observed.

Nothing could have been more calm and distinct than the voice of the Lord Jesus: 'Simon, son of John',

---

[1] See R. G. Trench, *Synonyms of the New Testament* (2000 ed.), p. 57.

he said, 'do you *love me* more than these?' (21:15). *More than these:* Do you love me more than these, your brethren, love me? Do you? Is your love for me stronger, purer, higher than theirs? Is it the noblest kind of love? That would stab Peter to the quick; his old weakness was to claim a superior kind of love and loyalty. Never, he had boasted, never would he fail as others might fail (*Mark* 14:29). But was his love in fact such a love that it could rise to so high a level? Shame and self-distrust made him shrink from a claim so far beyond his reach. He fell back to a more lowly level: 'Yes, Lord; you know that I love you.' The emphasis is decisive: it falls on the verb *love*, not on the pronoun *you*. It indicates an avoidance of the verb which Jesus had employed: 'I love you with such love as this poor heart can feel, even as a man loves his friend.'

No doubt there was a pause before the silence was broken with a further question. 'He said to him a second time, Simon, son of John, do you love me?' (21:16). There was a subtle movement in the line of thought: the phrase *more than these* had dropped out. So there was no longer any thought of comparison between Peter and the others. But the word *again* (AV, NASB, NIV) draws attention to the deliberate repetition of the same searching question. He chose the same verb as before without any comment on the lesser word employed by Peter. Simon, they heard him say, you are the man I love: do you love me like that? Have you made your choice and set your heart on me first and far above all? Peter loved him dearly in his own way, but would claim no more than he had before. *Yes, Lord:* words of earnest affirmation, 'Yes, Lord; you know that I love you' (21:16). But his love was on that lower level which spoke of the love of a man for his friend: it was like that of his brethren; it was warm and tender, but it was not more than theirs.

Again there was a pause: then once more for the last time a searching question: 'He said to him the third time, "Simon, son of John, do you love me?"' (21:17). But there was a further subtle change in the form of that question which the English text conceals: he dropped the verb which he had twice employed for the verb which Peter had chosen. He had come down to the level on which Peter stood in order to meet him on his own ground. I do not ask now, he seemed to say, if you love me with that most noble kind of love: what I ask is whether you love me with wholehearted affection even on a human level.

That was enough to touch the old wound on the raw. Peter could not hide his distress. 'Peter was grieved because he said unto him the third time, "Do you love me?"' (21:17). It was *the third time* of asking: this time even the kind of love he had ventured to claim was challenged. Peter was *grieved* because of this deliberate descent to his own self-chosen level. Could he in fact rightly claim even that humble form of love which he had avowed?

It was with a sadness almost too deep for words that he voiced his final reply: 'He said to him, "Lord, you know everything; you know that I love you"' (21:17). Peter had been deeply humbled as his inmost feelings had been probed and exposed. And now he dropped the words, *Yes, Lord*, for a preface of far greater solemnity. 'Lord', he said, 'you know everything'; all my shame, and all that is in my heart. And since the Lord knew all there was to know, he knew how much Peter loved him. And if his word for love was more lowly than the word first used by the Lord, it was only so by comparison, and in itself it still affirmed a word that was full of tender human feeling. That thrice repeated confession of love was as unique as his earlier confession of faith (*Matt.* 16:16), but was much more personal as a confession wrung from the depths of his soul. Peter would at length rise to the full glory of that higher kind of love in his words: 'Whom having not seen, ye love: in whom . . . ye rejoice greatly with joy unspeakable and full of glory' (1 *Pet.* 1:8, AV).

I can imagine no more searching challenge than to hear him ask, 'Do you love me?' One may hardly dare to claim more than Richard Baxter did in profound humility. 'Though I cannot say as thy apostle, thou knowest that I love thee; yet can I say, Lord, thou knowest that I *would* love thee.'[1]

Canon Charles Smyth quotes a saying from a book called *Ara Coeli:* 'Experience of God in this life means more than seeing a friend face to face, and less than seeing God face to face.' He went on to add his own fine comment: 'It is closer and more spiritual than the former, but more imperfect and fragmentary than the latter.'[2] One of Cowper's *Olney Hymns* was in the very spirit of Simon Peter's cry: it may not rate highly as poetry, but the chord it strikes is that of pure devotion.

> Lord, it is my chief complaint
> That my love is weak and faint;
> Yet I love Thee and adore:
> O for grace to love Thee more!

[1] Baxter, *The Saints' Everlasting Rest* (1652; repr. 1860), p. 630.
[2] Charles Smyth, *The Friendship of Christ* (1945), p. 10.

12

VIA CRUCIS, OR THE WAY OF THE CROSS

'This he said to show by what kind of death he was to glorify God' (John 21:19).

'Truly, truly, I say to you, when you were young, you used to dress yourself and walk wherever you wanted, but when you are old, you will stretch out your hands, and another will dress you and carry you where you do not want to go.' [19] (This he said to show by what kind of death he was to glorify God.) And after saying this he said to him, 'Follow me.' [20] Peter turned and saw the disciple whom Jesus loved following them, the one who had been reclining at table close to him and had said, 'Lord, who is it that is going to betray you?' [21] When Peter saw him, he said to Jesus, 'Lord, what about this man?' [22] Jesus said to him, 'If it is my will that he remain until I come, what is that to you? You follow me!' [23] So the saying spread abroad among the brothers that this disciple was not to die; yet Jesus did not say to him that he was not to die, but, 'If it is my will that he remain until I come, what is that to you?' [24] This is the disciple who is bearing witness about these things, and who has written these things, and we know that his testimony is true. [25] Now there are also many other things that Jesus did. Were every one of them to be written,

I suppose that the world itself could not contain
the books that would be written (*John* 21:18–25).

One might have thought that a final full stop
would stand at the end of verse 18, and there is
almost a sense of let-down when the conversation is
resumed. There was no change in the scene by the lake
as the sun began to climb over the hills; the boat had
been drawn up on the narrow margin of the shoreline.
The nets were there with the great haul of fish, and the
embers of the fire, and the remnants of the meal. The
seven disciples still stood in a semicircle face to face
with the Lord Jesus.

A fresh pause would follow Peter's reinstatement in
his Master's favour: then the Lord spoke again, in the
hearing of all, but with Peter in view. Peter had more
than once declared that he would go to prison and
death for his Master. 'Lord', he had said, 'why can I
not follow you now? I will lay down my life for you'
(*John* 13:37). He had no clear idea of all that this rash
and self-confident boast would entail.

But now the Lord told him that his promise would
be redeemed in full. The emphasis and gravity of the
opening formula was in keeping with the solemn

warning: 'Truly, truly, I say to you, when you were young, you used to dress yourself and walk wherever you wanted' (21:18). Peter had been born and bred to the free and independent life of the sea. He had sailed and fished at will and had just begun to taste those joys again. For him to think or to wish was to act and he rejoiced in youth and strength. *When you were young*, said Jesus: 'when you were even younger than you are now'.

Peter like the others was much of an age with Jesus himself, perhaps thirty-five years old at most. And as he stood on the beach that morning, he was still strong and free and in his prime. He could dress himself, as he had put on his outer garment out on the lake. He could go where he wanted, as when he had thrown himself into the sea. He could choose his own path and follow it with all the verve of early manhood. That was one side of the picture; but the freedom of youth would pass away.

The next words made it clear that Peter would not always be as he had been: 'But when you are old, you will stretch out your hands, and another will dress you and carry you where you do not want to go' (21:18). That was reminiscent of the words of David as he looked back over a long life and marked the contrast that age compels: 'I have been young, and now am old' (*Psa.* 37:25).

But the contrast between youth and age was only incidental to a greater contrast: the contrast between the freedom Peter had known as a young man and the restraint that old age would impose. The time would come when he could no longer do as he pleased, but would have to submit to the will of others. He would stretch out his hands as one who was helpless to stave off the hour of judgment. Someone else would dress him, load him with chains, bind him as a felon condemned and doomed: other hands would carry him where he would not have chosen of his own accord to go. Peter had been right as well as rash when he had promised, if need be, to die for Jesus: he had not known that old age would bring bonds and imprisonment and a violent martyrdom.

This led to an editorial comment to explain the meaning of those grave words: 'This he said to show by what kind of death he was to glorify God' (21:19). Those words may have had a very enigmatic ring in the ears of the men who heard them: but their significance had been made clear by the time when this account was written. Peter was told that he would die, but not the kind of death he would suffer; it was enough that he should know in broad terms what lay in store. There would be long years of service before he grew old, and then the crown of martyrdom.

And his understanding of this was clear in his encouragement to those who were called to suffer persecution. 'I think it right, as long as I am in this body, to stir you up by way of reminder, since I know that the putting off of my body will be soon, as our Lord Jesus Christ made clear to me' (2 *Pet.* 1:13–14). As long as he was free to choose, he would tread the path of faith and obedience. When he could no longer choose for himself, he would accept what God had planned for him.

The brief explanation was soon made and the narrative is once more resumed. 'And after saying this he said to him, "Follow me"' (*John* 21:19). Perhaps, having voiced that grave warning, Jesus turned round and began to move away: but as he did so, he called Peter to leave his friends by the fire and to follow. It was just the same call which had rung in his ears beside that lake so long before. But the old call would take on a new and larger meaning in the light of the Lord's death and resurrection.

Peter began to follow, thinking perhaps that there was more to be said in private, but the sound of footsteps behind made him turn round to see John who had also begun to follow. 'Lord', he exclaimed, 'what about this man?' (21:21). What will happen to him? Jesus knew which of the two would be taken early and which would long abide. But it was not for Peter to know what was in God's purpose for a fellow disciple. And his reply had a special solemnity: 'What is that to you? You *follow* me' (21:22).

It was Ambrose of Milan who preserved the story of what is now known as the *Quo Vadis* legend. Peter was in prison at Rome, under sentence of death, waiting for the day of execution. But friends implored him to seize the chance to escape: what would be wrong in that? Had not the Lord sent an angel to pluck him out of the hands of Herod? So he stole out through the prison doors to make once more for freedom, but as he passed through the city gate, he met the Lord who was on the way in. *'Domine'*, Peter cried, *'quo vadis?'* 'Lord, where are you going?' Peter was grieved at his reply: 'I go', the Lord said, 'to die in your place.' What could Peter do but return to his prison that he might glorify God by his death?

Did he die on the site where the Church of *S. Pietro* now stands? Was he crucified head downward? It may have been so, but it does not really matter: for us it is enough to know that the God of all grace had called him, after he had suffered awhile, to enter the eternal glory (see 1 *Pet.* 5:10).

13

EMMANUEL

'And behold, I am with you always, to the end of the age' (Matt. 28:20).

Now the eleven disciples went to Galilee, to the mountain to which Jesus had directed them. [17] And when they saw him they worshipped him, but some doubted. [18] And Jesus came and said to them, 'All authority in heaven and on earth has been given to me. [19] Go therefore and make disciples of all nations, baptizing them in the name of the Father and of the Son and of the Holy Spirit, [20] teaching them to observe all that I have commanded you. And behold, I am with you always, to the end of the age' (*Matt.* 28: 16–20).

The disciples had been told to make their way to Galilee: it was there that they would see him; so this was not a chance meeting: they had come to 'the mountain to which Jesus had directed them' (*Matt.* 28:16). Matthew spoke only of 'the eleven disciples', but they were not alone. This must have been the occasion when 'he appeared to more than five hundred brothers at once' (1 *Cor.* 15:6).

They came full of eager expectation: yet when they came, they were taken by surprise. The response was confused: 'When they saw him they worshipped him, but some doubted' (28:17). Was there something in his appearance, an aura of majesty, that left them in a quandary? But all doubt would vanish when he began to speak in terms of 'boundless magnificence'.[1] He who had once refused all the kingdoms of the world in return for a moment's homage had now received supreme authority over all things in heaven and on earth. Now he sent them to make disciples of all nations by baptism and instruction: 'And behold', he said, 'I am with you always, to the end of the age' (28:20).

---

[1] H. B. Swete: *The Appearances of Our Lord after the Passion* (2nd edition, 1908), pp. 69–70.

And behold: a word that would alert them to the momentous character of what came next: 'And behold, I am with you always': even, that is, until the end of time. They were to go into 'all the world' (*Mark* 16:15), to 'the remotest part of the earth' (*Acts* 1:8, NASB). But then, lest the command, *Go,* should seem too hard, he told them he would be with them.

How were they to understand this? How did it square with what he had said before? 'The poor you always have with you, but you do not always have me' (*John* 12:8). He had spoken freely on the eve of his death of the fact that he was soon to 'go away' (see also *John* 16:7).

Death would remove him from their midst and his presence in the body would be withdrawn. He would ascend to the right hand of God and his body could only be in one place at one time. But there are no limitations to his presence by means of his Spirit in the heart of those who love him. Thus the warning, 'You do not always have me', is matched by the promise, 'I am with you always.' And those who go where he would have them go, will have him with them wherever they go.

Always: there is something sweet and something grand in that word as it falls on our ears. And it reminds us how often God has assured now this man, now that man, that he would be with him.

Jacob as a fugitive from his family, asleep in the desert, a stone for his pillow, the sky for a ceiling, heard God's voice in his dream, 'Behold, I am with you' *(Gen. 28:15)*.

Moses, as an exile from the court of Egypt, at the west side of the desert, saw a bush on fire that was not consumed and heard God say: 'Certainly I will be with you' (*Exod.* 3:12).

When the Christ-child was born, his name was called Emmanuel: 'The God who is with us.' And when the hour came for him to ascend, that great promise was caught up in words of sovereign finality.

That has been the strength and support of God's servants from generation to generation. For the promise of his presence was not confined to the first disciples of the first century. It would stretch far into the future and would reach to the ends of the earth. 'For this God is our God for ever and ever: he will be our guide even unto death' (*Psa.* 48:14, AV).

The end: a word that points to the consummation of the whole created universe, 'to the end of the age', even, that is, till time shall be no more. The quiet language of the Authorized Version hides the technical character of this phrase: but the rendering of the English Standard Version makes it clear that 'the consummation of the age' is meant. Jesus would soon return to that glory which had been his before the world was made. He would be lost to sight and seen no more of men until he rends the veil to come again. They were henceforth to walk by faith, 'as seeing him who is invisible' (*Heb.* 11:27). But they would not be deprived of the strength and comfort of his presence.

They would live in a world of change; little that they knew would remain the same. But he who died on the cross and rose from the grave is forever 'this same Jesus'. All that he was yesterday, he is today. All that he is today, he will be forever. He will never fail or forsake those whose trust is in him; never let them down; never let them go.

Amen: that word rings out at the close of this verse in the Authorized Version. But it does not belong to the Greek text; it was added by a nameless scribe in heartfelt assent. It was like the first sound of the trumpet with the end of the age in sight: for the promise that he would be with them would reach to the final triumph of the gospel.

That day may well have seemed infinitely remote to those wondering disciples. But all authority belongs to him: he is almighty; he must reign; and he is with us. He is just as truly with his people now as when he stood on that mountain overlooking the lake of Galilee. He will be with them each day, and all the days, until he comes in his glory. To have him with them would be better than to have twelve legions of angels at their back. It would nerve their arm with strength and their soul with hope to the utmost limit of time and need.

And as for people like ourselves, that golden word of promise is all we could desire. So that like that nameless scribe, we add our own joyful *Amen!* So be it, Lord!

This was David Livingstone's text. One hot summer night, in the heart of darkest Africa, he found himself hemmed in by a cordon of wild and savage tribesmen. Sixteen years he had been in Africa, and never in such peril before. For the first time he felt tempted to steal away and seek safety in flight. But he laid his finger once more on those words of promise in the Bible: 'And lo, I am with you alway, even unto the end of the world.'

He copied that promise in his journal and heavily underlined it. 'It is the word of a Gentleman of the most strict and sacred honour', he wrote; 'so there's an end of it, I will not cross furtively tonight as I intended . . . I feel quite calm now, thank God.'

Later that year he went home to Scotland, but in due course announced his resolve to return. A great hush fell on his hearers as he told them how he would go back in the strength of that promise: 'For', he said, 'on those words I staked everything, and they never failed.'

14

OLIVET

'Then he led them out as far as Bethany'
(Luke 24:50).

Then he led them out as far as Bethany, and lifting up his hands he blessed them. [51] While he blessed them, he parted from them and was carried up into heaven (*Luke* 25:50–53).

In the first book, O Theophilus, I have dealt with all that Jesus began to do and teach, [2] until the day when he was taken up, after he had given commands through the Holy Spirit to the apostles whom he had chosen. [3] To them he presented himself alive after his suffering by many proofs, appearing to them during forty days and speaking about the kingdom of God. [4] And while staying with them he ordered them not to depart from Jerusalem, but to wait for the promise of the Father, which, he said, 'you heard from me; [5] for John baptized with water, but you will be baptized with the Holy Spirit not many days from now.' [6] So when they had come together, they asked him, 'Lord, will you at this time restore the kingdom to Israel?' [7] He said to them, 'It is not for you to know times or seasons that the Father has fixed by his own authority. [8] But you will receive power when the Holy Spirit has come upon you, and you will be my witnesses in Jerusalem and in all Judea and Samaria, and to the end of the earth.' ⁹ And when he had said these things, as they were looking on, he was lifted up, and a cloud took him out of their sight (*Acts* 1:1–9).

Luke stands alone as the only Evangelist to describe the Ascension from Olivet. And his record in the Gospel and in the Acts is still full of haunting beauty. The one other verse in the Gospels to speak of this event is more like a credal statement: 'So then the Lord Jesus . . . was taken up into heaven and sat down at the right hand of God' (*Mark* 16:19).

Forty days had come and gone since he had burst the bands of death to rise again: days in which he had 'presented himself alive' (*Acts* 1:3), both in Judea and in Galilee. He had furnished 'many other signs' as proof of his resurrection reality as the Son of God (*John* 20:30). He had appeared to the disciples from time to time in ones or twos or in larger groups. He had given them his last instructions with regard to the kingdom of God. And after each encounter he had simply vanished, they knew not where. But the hour had now come when he would see them and leave them for the last time. Such an event would be unique: the whole character of the Ascension was stamped with finality.

The disciples had travelled south from Galilee and he met them once more in Jerusalem. 'Then he led them out as far as Bethany', just like the days of old.

On the eve of his death he had led them down to the brook Kidron and on to Gethsemane. Now he followed the same path, but on beyond Gethsemane to climb the Mount of Olives. There he could look to the west where Jerusalem lay spread before his eyes. Or he could look to the east over the desolate wilderness to the far distant mountains of Moab. They came to a halt in a fold of the hills, *over against* the village of Bethany. They were near enough to look in that direction, but far enough to preserve their solitude. This was the only occasion after the resurrection when he led them from place to place. It was like the last journey of Elijah from Gilgal to Bethel, from Bethel to Jericho, from Jericho to Jordan. Did the disciples know as Elisha knew that God would take away their Head that day? Would they long like Elisha for a double portion of his Spirit at his going?

Their last conversation was taken up with a question which they ventured to ask: 'Lord,' they inquired, 'will you at this time restore the kingdom to Israel?'

(*Acts* 1:6). They were obsessed with their dream of worldly splendour in an earthly kingdom; would he wrest the crown from Caesar in Rome and set up his throne in Jerusalem? They had always cherished the hope that he was the one who would redeem Israel (*Luke* 24:21). And they could not grasp the truth that his kingdom was not of this world (*John* 18:36).

Jesus did not offer any further comment on their lack of understanding. 'It is not for you', he said, 'to know times or seasons that the Father has fixed by his own authority' (*Acts* 1:7). Their duty was to wait in Jerusalem until they were 'clothed with power from on high' (*Luke* 24:49).

Then they were to go forth and bear witness to his name, even to the ends of the earth. The compass would open out from Jerusalem as its centre to the furthest parts of the world. Nor would their mission be complete until those far off parts had been possessed for him.

That was his last recorded utterance and it was still fresh in their minds when they came to a halt, 'and lifting up his hands he blessed them' (*Luke* 24:50). They would gather in a little semi-circle so as to stand face to face with the Lord: and what followed made them finally aware that this was the moment of farewell.

When Jacob was dying, his twelve sons came before him to receive his blessing. And when Moses addressed his farewell to Israel, he blessed each of the twelve tribes in turn. So now Jesus, *lifting up his hands*, those hands which had been nailed to the cross. The print of the nails in his hands was the pledge of a love that had no equal. His very first action on the resurrection evening had been to show them his hands; and now his last gesture as he was about to leave them was to lift up those hands in blessing. J. C. Ryle said that he had come to bless, and not to curse, and blessing he would go away; he had come in mercy, and not in wrath, and in mercy he would go to his Father.[1]

His hands were still upraised in the act of blessing when he began to ascend in glory: 'While he blessed them, he parted from them and was carried up into heaven' (24:51).

There is always sweet sorrow in parting; but how would this parting take place? It would be with infinite gentleness, while he was yet in the very act of blessing. Nothing would be less like what had happened on all previous occasions when he had just vanished; now there was a slow and deliberate ascent, accompanied by

[1] J. C. Ryle, *Expository Thoughts on Luke* (1858; repr. Edinburgh: Banner of Truth, 1986), vol. 2, p. 525.

an impressive majesty. He was *lifted up* (*Acts* 1:9): he *parted* from them (*Luke* 24:51): he was *carried up* into heaven (24:51). It was as though there were an unseen arm that caught him up before their very eyes.

The verbs in the Gospel and in the Acts describe the whole movement rather than its details. They watched him *as he went* (*Acts* 1:10) until a cloud took him out of their sight. There was no sudden rapture, no fiery chariot, as there had been in the case of Elijah. He went up in full view of the eleven disciples until he passed beyond the point of sight.

The last sight that mortal eyes were allowed was as he went in that trail of glory. Once that cloud hid him from their eyes, they knew that he had been *taken* into heaven. Perhaps no one else saw that cloud as it spread its shadow over them on the Mount of Olives.

It was that special cloud which had overshadowed him on the Mount of Transfiguration. Such a cloud had once been the sign of God's presence in the desert with his people. It was allowed to rest on the tabernacle as a token of the glory that dwelt within. Human eyes could not see beyond the cloud where the angel host was waiting as an escort.

But a Messianic Psalm fills out the picture as he went up in glory to glory. No ear on earth heard the shout of triumph at the golden gates of heaven: 'Lift up your heads, O gates! And lift them up, O ancient doors, that the King of glory may come in' (*Psa.* 24:9).

And then he passed 'through the heavens' (*Heb.* 4:14), 'sat down at the right hand of the Majesty on high' (*Heb.* 1:3) and was 'crowned with glory and honour' (*Heb.* 2:9), risen, ascended, glorified.

15

MARAN-ATHA

'This same Jesus . . . shall so come in like manner as ye have seen him go' (Acts 1:11, AV).

And while they were gazing into heaven as he went, behold, two men stood by them in white robes, [11] and said, 'Men of Galilee, why do you stand looking into heaven? This Jesus, who was taken up from you into heaven, will come in the same way as you saw him go into heaven' (*Acts* 1:10–11).

And they worshipped him and returned to Jerusalem with great joy, [53] and were continually in the temple blessing God (*Luke* 24:52–53).

The disciples on Olivet were left standing there in silent awe and wonder, lost in artless desire to pierce beyond the cloud which had received him out of sight. Their long lingering upward gaze, long after gazing had become useless, was all very human. It spoke of their hope that the cloud would soon dissolve and leave him with them as before.

How long they stood like that, we are not told; but such a hope would be in vain. 'And while they were gazing into heaven as he went, behold, two men stood by them in white robes' (*Acts* 1:10). These two correspond with the 'two men . . . in shining garments' outside the empty tomb (*Luke* 24:4, AV). They had asked the searching question: 'Why do you seek the living among the dead?' (24:5).

So these two were angels who came to greet and cheer them with words of comfort. And they also began with a question: 'Men of Galilee, why do you stand looking into heaven?' (*Acts* 1:11). *Galilee,* whence they had come, was in pointed contrast with *heaven,* where he had gone. But *why* did they go on standing there? Did they not know that God had some better plan for them?

Their sense of loss was met with reassurance and consolation full of kindness. 'This Jesus' – 'This same Jesus' (AV) – 'who was taken up from you into heaven' (1:11). The whole scene had been steeped both in mystery and in majesty as it took place before their eyes. These disciples from Galilee had no intuitive explanation for an event that was truly unique. There was no room for doubt as to what had happened; they could hardly deny what they had seen. He had been *taken up* in his risen body as though the law of gravity did not exist.

He had vanished from their midst on various occasions with a surprising suddenness. Nor had they known where or how he went when they found themselves alone. But now they could only marvel at this calm and sublime ascent before their eyes. It would take time before they could fully absorb or easily interpret what it all meant. The Lord Jesus had gone from one sphere of being to another that is beyond all that they could conceive: 'He who descended is *the one who also* ascended far above all the heavens' (*Eph.* 4:10).

The last sight the disciples had of the Lord Jesus was as that cloud enveloped him. They saw him as he was going, as he was on his way; they could not see beyond the cloud. It was only when the angels told them that they knew that he had gone 'into heaven'.

Heaven: four times in two verses that word would be used in this account of the Ascension. The disciples had stood *gazing into heaven*: they were steadily looking towards the sky; but there was a scarcely noticed and subtle change in meaning when he was said to be taken 'into heaven'. What did that word mean in this new context? Where was the heaven into which he was taken? Were they meant to think of somewhere far off in space above the bright blue sky?

Men can only think or speak of heaven with the aid of picture language. He had come down from heaven to earth at Bethlehem; he went up from earth to heaven at Olivet. Heaven is where God is: he is 'our Father in heaven'. Jesus is there with him, at his right hand.

However little the disciples understood, they knew that in heaven he was crowned with glory. That long wistful gaze was answered by a promise far beyond all their dreams: 'This Jesus . . . *will come in the same way* as you saw him go into heaven' (1:11). It was not said that they would go to him, but that he would come to them. And that told them that this separation was both final, and not final.

It was final in the sense that they would regard him no longer after the flesh: yet not final in as much as they were now told that he would come again. There would be no loss of identity between his going away and coming again: and the reassurance that it will be *this same Jesus* who will come cannot be overstated. That promise has been the strength and hope of the church all down the ages. It has shed a special light on the saints of God in the darkest days of persecution. And it provides the strongest incentive to pursue a life of personal holiness. 'Beloved . . . what we will be has not yet appeared; but we know that when he appears we shall be like him, because we shall see him as he is' (1 *John* 3:2).

The promise of his return was firmly anchored to the drama of his Ascension. *In the same way:* as they saw him ascend so will we see him when he comes again. This is the most precise statement in the New Testament on the nature of his return. And that return is seen as the sequel to the resurrection and its aftermath.

Did he rise in body? Then in body he will return, and not as a spirit. Did he come in person? Then in person he will return, and not as a phantom. Did he ascend in glory? Then *in the same way* he will come again. And the glory of his return will be tenfold greater than the glory of his going. Did a cloud take him out of their sight? He will come with trailing clouds of glory. Were the angels there as his escort? All the angels of God will be with him when he comes again. Did disciples from Galilee with eyes full of wonder and worship follow him as he went up? He will come 'on that day to be glorified in his saints, and to be marvelled at among all who have believed' (2 *Thess.* 1:10).

No idea of sadness cast its shadow over the disciples on Olivet. 'Then they returned to Jerusalem from the mount called Olivet, which is near Jerusalem, a Sabbath day's journey away' (*Acts* 1:12). They would retrace their steps over some six furlongs of a winding path to Jerusalem.

And one or two extra details in the Gospel account round off the story. 'And they worshipped him and returned to Jerusalem with great joy, and were continually in the temple blessing God' (*Luke* 24:52–53). They had gone back to the city in which he had been condemned and crucified.

But they were unafraid: joy filled their hearts; worship and praise prevailed. They knew that they would see him no more as in the days of old, but if they had seen him go in grace and glory, they knew that in power and glory he would come again.

Henceforth they would adopt as their watchword the old Aramaic saying, 'Maran-atha': 'Our Lord, come!' (1 *Cor.* 16:22). 'Amen: Even so, come, Lord Jesus' (*Rev.* 22:20, AV).

OTHER TITLES FROM THE
BANNER OF TRUTH
TRUST

Marcus L. Loane

MASTERS OF THE
ENGLISH REFORMATION

The story of the English Reformation is told here, less as a movement of political and religious change than as the result of a hidden work of the Spirit of God in men of humble heart and heroic faith.

The five men chosen for this study (Thomas Bilney, William Tyndale, Hugh Latimer, Nicholas Ridley, and Thomas Cranmer) were perhaps the most significant of those who laid down their lives in the cause of Christ in England between the 1530s and the 1550s.

Both a serious study and a gripping narrative, this is a work which, page by page, communicates to the reader the writer's enthusiasm for the spiritual convictions of the five men described.

'In a style full of pathos . . . Loane captures the spirit of the Reformers in 300 captivating pages.'

REFORMED THEOLOGICAL REVIEW

'A work that will both inform and inspire.'

Australian Presbyterian

'The Reformers' labours and sufferings are so percep-
tively and vividly portrayed that the sympathetic reader is
made to relive these momentous times.'

Peace and Truth

'Ought to be found in every Christian home . . . leaves
one greatly humbled and silent with amazement and
admiration.'

English Churchman

'Brings out vividly the drama, dynamism and inspir-
ation of the sixteenth century . . . very readable.'

Evangelicals Now

'A challenging and stirring book which will be a blessing to all who read it.'

Free Church Witness

'Brings these men to life . . . full of challenge and
instruction.'

Covenanter Witness

320 pp., clothbound, illustrated
ISBN 0 85151 910 5

MARCUS L. LOANE

THEY WERE PILGRIMS

This is the fascinating story of four remarkable men who shared a common spiritual aim and ideal—David Brainerd, Henry Martyn, Robert Murray M'Cheyne, and Ion Keith-Falconer. Their average life-span was only thirty years, but they left a spiritual impact on their generation which was altogether out of the ordinary.

A clear line of spiritual descent can be traced from David Brainerd to Henry Martyn, from Brainerd and Martyn to Robert Murray M'Cheyne, and from Martyn to Ion Keith-Falconer. They were all pioneers in the missionary movement: Brainerd with the Native North Americans, M'Cheyne with the Jews of Palestine and Central Europe, Martyn and Keith-Falconer in the Muslim world of Persia and Arabia.

'This handsome new edition [will] inspire, challenge and encourage us to a deeper devotion to Jesus Christ.'
GOSPEL MAGAZINE

'Loane makes these men come alive and challenges our devotion and commitment to making Christ known.'
EVANGELICALS NOW

'Marcus Loane's poetic and romantic streak provides colour and dimension in these portraits of four men who were inspired by a passionate loyalty to the lordship of Christ and to the spread of the gospel.'
PROTESTANT TRUTH

'The testimonies of these four great men live on in this book, speaking to a new generation and bringing a challenge for today.'
BRITISH CHURCH NEWSPAPER

'This fascinating and encouraging book [should] whet our appetite for personal holiness and stir us to increased service.'
GRACE MAGAZINE

272 pp., clothbound, illustrated
ISBN 0 85151 928 8

EDWARD DONNELLY

PETER: EYEWITNESS
OF HIS MAJESTY

This outstanding study of Peter shows how the grace of God moulded the penitent disciple we meet at the close of the Gospel accounts (see especially chapters 4 and 11 of the present work by Marcus Loane) into a mighty preacher and apostle, so that, in the words of Albert N. Martin, the rough-hewn Galilean fisherman was fashioned into 'a polished instrument in the hands of the Master'.

'Heart-warming, challenging, scholarly and comprehensive . . . this work is clearly written from a pastor's heart for the people of God and the servants of Christ.'

EVANGELICAL PRESBYTERIAN

'Non-technical and easily read, this study ultimately centres our thoughts more on Peter's Lord than on Peter —exactly as Peter would have wanted it.'

REFORMED THEOLOGICAL JOURNAL

'Makes the apostle Peter come alive. Very readable and full of spiritual counsel and uplift, as well as solid teaching.'

GOSPEL MAGAZINE

'A wealth of sound biblical advice and encouragement . . . anyone involved in regular preaching and pastoral ministry would greatly profit from this book.'

EVANGEL

'A most humbling and enriching book.'

COVENANTER WITNESS

'Characterized by warmth and faithfulness to the Scriptures.'

MONTHLY RECORD

160 pp., large paperback
ISBN 0 85151 744 7

For free illustrated catalogue please write to
THE BANNER OF TRUTH TRUST

3 Murrayfield Road,   P O Box 621, Carlisle,
Edinburgh EH12 6EL   Pennsylvania 17013,
UK   USA

www.banneroftruth.co.uk